Praise for

FOUNDATION

"Father told me I should never cry. / What a thing to demand of a waterfall." A tender, expansive meditation on masculinity and grief, absence and belonging, Gustavo Barahona-Lopez' *Foundation* is a work rooted in the heart of the bordered body. Speaking as both child and father, memory and witness, the future and the past, Barahona-Lopez's poems strike a chord between searing critique and bright compassion, engaged in the reparative act of radical imagining.

—**Vanessa Angélica Villarreal**, author of *Beast Meridian*

Gustavo Barahona-Lopez gives texture and substance to our dreams, our heartbreaks, our anger, and our wonder. Through cobblestones, smokestacks, cartilage, lakes, and tears, Barahona-Lopez gives language to our unspeakable truths. How do we reckon with the fathers that love us in beautiful and sometimes hurtful ways? What do we do when our histories and lineages are interrupted or otherwise hidden by migration? *Foundation* is a book I will cherish for a long time.

—**José Olivarez**, author of *Promises of Gold*

In these marvelous and moving poems, the speaker molds his own blood, builds upon a 'corroded base.' An elegiac but defiant tone ripples through the book: tenderness pivots to anger, bewilderedness dovetails into wonder. Gustavo Barahona-Lopez's language—resonant, lyrical— constructs a space where his speaker can tend to his wounds, inhabit a present rich with possibilities.

—**Eduardo Corral**, author of *Slow Lightning*

"They call us locusts forgetting how we have fed them" -- Daaaamn. This line has stayed with me from the first 'speed-read' through the close read. I love how it works in multiple contexts: as fieldworkers feeding the ppl, or as perhaps a subtle, guess what fools, we've been feeding the locusts and they might be coming for YOU now.

—**Anthody Cody**, author of *Borderland Apocrypha*

FOUNDATION

Gustavo Barahona-López

WINNER OF THE
CHICANX VISIONS BOOK SERIES

FLOWERSONG
PRESS

FlowerSong Press
Copyright © 2025 by Gustavo Barahona-López
ISBN: 978-1-963245-24-0

Published by FlowerSong Press
in the United States of America.
www.flowersongpress.com

Author Photo by Adrian Romero
Cover Art by Sofia Moreno

Set in Adobe Garamond Pro

NOTICE: SCHOOLS AND BUSINESSES
FlowerSong Press offers copies of this book at quantity discount with
bulk purchase for educational, business, or sales promotional use. For
information, please email the Publisher at info@flowersongpress.com.

FOUNDATION

FLOWERSONG
PRESS

poems by

Gustavo Barahona-López

FLOWERSONG
P R E S S

**Winner of the inaugural
Chicanx Visions Book Series
Project Prize**

table of contents

I

II

III

About the
Chicanx Visions Book Series:

This project is possible through the Gente Chicana/SOYmos Chicanos Fund. Grants from this fund shall be used to support the understanding, appreciation and practice of Chicano/na Art.

FlowerSong Press believes that it is important to promote Chicanx poetry and writing. Chicanx poetry has always been about both celebration and protest: celebrating Chicanx culture and people, and continuing to fight injustice. Even though it's been almost 60 years since *Yo Soy Joaquin* entered the world, the same issues that epic addresses are still present in the world. It is necessary for Chicanx art to be produced because it is necessary that Chicanx speak about/to the world and their place in it.

FOUNDATION

I

Chevron Check Ghazal

Hydrocarbon cloud fires itself into a new existence, a type of life
Brought about by its own destruction. All my early life

I grew in the shadow of smokestacks, smog misting thirsty earth.
The running juices of lemons and tomatoes made a worthy life.

My father applied his calloused hands to cultivate our backyard,
Proudly served bowls of sliced peaches. His love language. His life

Was cut short. He, like my uncles, like myself, is a statistic.
Elevated cancer and asthma rates the reward for taking life-

Giving breath. How much death is ingested in the name of survival?
Like crude oil, the years continue to leak from my shortened life.

One day my mother boiled chayotes she'd grown. I devoured their
Spiny hearts, an incantation to rid me of the poison threatening my life.

Today I tender the corrosion nesting in my lungs. I cash a $300 check
From the latest Chevron settlement and consider the value of this life.

How to Make a Man

At conception, conjure
the masculine with will.
Declare, *My son*
was the biggest
baby born at the hospital
today.

Close the blinds
of your home, mistrust
burrows like screw-
worms into flesh.

Tell your son
he is useless
just enough for him
to believe. Turn
his skin to leather.
An artisan, you
crosshatch soft hands.

Destabilize his world
like a blown
tire, rims sparking
on asphalt leave a trail
of wildfires.

Compose him
stories. Build entire worlds.
Myth: *I once beat a gym*

rat for talking shit. Jacked
abs didn't save the bastard
from my fist.

Instruct: *Restrain manhood*
like a fish. Put your thumb inside
its mouth. Let it bite
down, draw blood.
Repeat.

Refuse to look him
in the face when he threatens
to cry. After all
you learned to cope
by being beaten
by an alcoholic father.

Ask your son, *How*
many girls are you dating?
When you know
the answer. Then
remind him of how you
had three girlfriends
in two countries.

And one night
when you've had too
many beers,
apologize
for the man
each of you
has become.

Bloodbending

When I was   born   I refused to open
          my eyes.   The light
                    too piercing.   Glaciers   formed   around
                              my pupils,
threatened   to shipwreck.
                    My parents'   imagination   plunged
into those   chromosomes   as if they added
          mass   to my existence.   My mother
               laments   when her genes
dominate   my father's.   She sees herself
          in my brother's   copper rings.   Would she rip   apart
                    the nucleotides   that tie him   to her?
What is a body   other than   a river
          contained?   I follow   the path
          of the   moon climbing   from zero-
point   to zero   point.   My hands
          grasping,   molding   my blood.

Waterfall Duplex

Father told me I should never cry.
What a thing to demand of a waterfall.

       I cannot ask more of myself, a waterfall.
       He tells me he almost drowned in a lake.

Whirlpool nearly drowned him in a lake.
Part of my father resides in the water.

       I've learned to reside in my own water.
       Shutting out light reminds me of home.

Father kept out the sunlight at home.
Who, I wonder, was he hiding from?

       I can't name the fears I am hiding from.
       Father spits blood into a plastic cup.

Writing a poem, I give him his bloody cup.
I recite my poem. We both begin to cry.

Crows Hold Grudges For Generations

Some days I wonder what crows
squawk about, what it'd be like
to caress their dark
feathers like a bouquet
of baby's breath.
I think they are talking shit
about me.
How my hair is not black,
like I deceived
myself into believing,
but dark brown.
Brown as in body
breached.
Body as in wings
severed. My wings
are marinated in buffalo
sauce, teeth nibble on
cartilage as tongue extracts
morsels between bones.
I fear my ancestors
will not recognize me.
How many languages have I lost?
I, of the impoverished lexicon,
watch words pop
like bubbles after kissing
blades of grass. I am

much too fractured
to believe in bygones.
I am too much earth to die.

Self Portrait as Blank Name Tag

I do not question why my classmates
are standing around my bed
wearing jeans and t-shirts
by designers I do not know.
My soccer team runs by but
I feel it would be improper to join them
given I have no cleats on.
Instead, since no one seems phased
by the fact I am in my flannel pajamas,
I contort my body to make myself
seem as at ease as they are.
A girl from my advising group
comes up to me and asks
for me to say my full name.
Gustavo Adolfo Barahona-López,
I deliver, not bothering to anglicize shit.
With a satisfied giggle she turns and walks
away from me. I see a guy from my Calculus class
and remember I owe him a dollar I used
to buy a Coke. Panicked, I reach for
my non-existent pockets.
My mother once told me,
Always pay your debts promptly.
My mother often told me,
California was stolen from México in 1848.
Who then is the debtor?

My head begins to hang. I can no longer
keep my eyes from shutting out their faces.
I wrap myself in my golden eagle-clad blanket,
its talons facing outwards.

About a Horse, Dear Reader, About a Horse

My uncle put the saddle on the horse.
Its jaws were constrained by a reign.
I rejoiced at having control
over our path.
I could make the horse change
direction with merely a pull
or a tug.
As I sat on the saddle, my sombrero
projected a shadow on my shirt
emblazoned with
the Dallas Cowboys logo.
I smacked the horse and
it began to move.
I tugged at the reign to no avail.
The horse went under a tree,
the branches slashed at my arms.
I got off the horse and checked
for wounds.
My cowboy shirt was torn.

My Grandfather, the one with the dog that almost bit me, the one who died of prostate cancer

Atacheo, Michoacán, México
my town, my parents' town, my grandparents' town
there lived a man who loved dogs
had ten sons and daughters
died in the house his son built
died on 9/11
Que descanse en paz mi abuelito.

He always knew what to do
spent it all on beer
believed in God:
smote those who disobeyed
Que descanse en paz, mi pobre abuelito.

I did not know him well
except through my father's authority
Que descanse en paz mi abuelito.

His dog, once killed a giant rat
barked and almost bit me;
was punished
died of poison meant for the rats
Que descanse en paz, mi pobre abuelito.

I am his grandson
the one that caught his chickens
no longer the future of the family name
I have to work, he tells me
God, let my grandfather rest in peace.

Kallio, the Sunken Village

I walk into a ghost village.
  Water half lives in buildings
that once recorded
   the transitory. You see,
      for all its movement,
    even a man-made
lake holds onto eternity
    like it is a coin begging to be flipped.
I stare in emerald waves
    swaddle piles of stones
       that perhaps once made a wall,
     perhaps a home. Now
       a rearticulated sand.
   At what point does a lake
      cease to be
       artificial?
    When is it purely body?
   The permanent
    recalls a launch
       into itself.
    Cerulean cloud
  chastens me.
  I make out sets of five petals
surrounding a golden halo.
   I bite my tongue.
     Atonement made tangible.
  My blood outgrows my body,
     becomes water.

It spatters on green rock,
                disappears. How do I
                                taste? I wonder
            why so many gods
                    chose to make us out of clay,
    mud to be breathed
            into being. After all,
                    even stones have a half-life.

Looking

for you
in the shadows
of the world
including my own

you are
the elusive
whisper that
once
found
engulfs
me a spinning
haze of brightness
startled truth
do not let go
until I scribble
my soul
on canvas

come to me
grant
me the moment
of clarity
your embrace

Mi Padre, el más fuerte del mundo

Mi padre trabajó desde los cinco años
Trabajó para mantener a sus hermanos
Sobrevivió lo más duro de la vida
Cruzó al país de oportunidad
Se casó con una de sus muchas seguidoras
Con mi mamá
Trabajó para asegurar nuestro futuro
Quedó deshabilitado en el trabajo

Mi padre es una indomable fuerza
Con un poder infinito
Con una mente de genio
Lo único que le faltó fue oportunidad
Que este país no le brindo,
Pero que ahora me brinda a mí

Aunque estaba deshabilitado
Podía noquear a cualquiera
Hasta al mismo Julio César Chávez
Yo trato de describir su grandeza
Pero no creo que sea posible hacerlo
Pero este es un esfuerzo

Nací idéntico
Su reencarnación en vida
Un clon
Un hermano gemelo
Menor por tan solo unas décadas
Los mismos ojos, el mismo pelo

La misma mente
El mismo amor por la familia
Pudo haber sido grande
Pudo haber sido casi un Dios
En ojos estadounidenses
Pero tuvo que trabajar por su familia amada
Padre, mi guía-Padre, mi Dios
Lo amamos por ello

95 por ciento cáncer, páncreas
Hijo de Dios
Seguidor bendito
Se me va porque es necesitado en lo más alto del cielo
Se me va porque lo necesita Dios

My Father, the strongest in the world

My father worked since he was five years old
Working to support his family
He survived the hardships of life
Crossed into the land of opportunity
Married one of his many admirers
Married my mom
He worked to secure our future
He became disabled at work

My father is an indomitable force
With the mind of a genius
The only thing he needed was opportunity
Which this country did not offer him
But now offers to me

Even though he was disabled
He could knock out anyone
Even Julio César Chávez
I try to describe his greatness
But I don't think it is possible
But this is an attempt

I was born
His clone
Younger by only a few decades
The same eyes, the same hair
The same mind
The same love for our family
He could have been great

He could have been nearly a God
In American eyes
But he had to work for his beloved family
Father, my guide-Father, my God
We love him for it

95 percent pancreatic cancer
Son of God
Divine follower
I am losing him because he is needed in the greatest heights of
heaven
I am losing him because God needs him

Navigate My Consciousness

Like shattered heart.
Its angles a series of spears,
No ring, no games.
My cells split
Trauma to
The subatomic. Test:

How does the cult
Of behavior escape
Fracture? Depression

As a casual moth.
It carries my flaws
Like a box of trinkets.

I bathe
In a deep tangle of milk.
Acoustic moons reflect
My crossings.

Green, How I Want You

My father once raised plants for a living
He carried flower beds
Carnations lilacs peonies
Water fertilizer dirt
The flower beds broke him
The carrying cracked his spinal chord
The flowers swallowed the tender in him
Drank the dancing in him

      *   *   *

My mother fell in love
With my father dancing
She has a green thumb
To be clear
Petals are her fertilizer
Blooming her joy
My father threw her blooming
Onto concrete
Cracked pots broken roots
His fingers around her neck
Like a vine so green so green

      *   *   *

I sprouted without light
Without the carrying
There was so much blooming

The red the fire the thorn
The belt the rod the vitriol
My bruises bloomed purple
Then green

*   *   *

Vines embedded themselves
In my veins roots snaked through
My capillaries until they broke skin
How do I call myself a garden?
Green, how I want you green
Every day a new leaf a new sprout
Every day a small green death

I Tried to Give You my Star

You said if I ever made a star
you'd nurture its light.
You said it was all
you ever wanted.
You said make it so.

So, when I plucked a star
from inside my throat
and called it rosemary,
forgive me for wanting
to share its overwhelming
radiance with you.

Forgive that my little star
was still covered in my blood,
which is to say your blood.
Forgive that I expected you
to give it your devotion.

You see, from the moment
I plucked the star
out of my body, I knew
I had been given a new life.

I had to become a sun to teach
my star how to be incandescent.
You, however, could not look
into the brightness for long.

You must know how much I wanted
to bring you into the light.
You must know I can no longer
stand with you in the dark.

II

Foundation

I.

November 18, 1993
I have seen Time Magazine's "The New Face
Of America" before. She is my sister
Or my cousin or that distant auntie.
The auntie that calls indígenas savages.
America is computer-generated familial,
Morphing to create the kind of offspring
That can eat the sun whole. Her eyes
Sing an egalitarian promise but
I know when she lies. The nation
Desires brown flesh only as long
As it remains theoretical, like a costume
It uses to scare itself in the mirror.
Rejected, I used to obsess over Aztec
Deities as if they could quell my hunger
For place. Mestizaje offered fortification
From empire with empire. But when I spoke
To my mother about Coatlicue, she
Could not see herself in the earth,
Prayed to the Virgen de Guadalupe instead.
If only my ancestors still talked to me.
Perhaps I would not be at the whim
Of reimagined nationhood.

II.

DNA test tries to tell me I am not who I imagined myself to be.
Percentage points are allotted to scattered kin who may or may not
know I exist. Continents pangea into one another like a collapsing
star. The gods I was supposed to worship dance upon my cartography.
The God I learned to worship becomes ink. Catholicism drips from
my map like a stain. I trace voyages along oceans, chart the trails that
allegedly led to my conception. I never take a DNA test.

III.

My past holds
             Too many secrets.
                          I will never hear.
A story
             Of silences
                          Subdued.

             Where do I come from?
A breath.
                          A breaking.
A dream   Realized.

             I am a place
             Reaching
                          For its own foundation.

IV.

Please forgive me for forgetting
             That which I never witnessed,
Myths I was never told. I know

I've been a bad son but
Remember I am but a pebble thrown
     Into the time river.
I can build a dam but not alone. I can
     Remake myself but not alone.
I will not speak for you. I haven't
     The right to. You do not know
Who I am, perhaps you know exactly
     Where I've been. I welcome you
Into the caverns within me. Be sure
     Not to get lost among the crystals.
I want to anchor my dream of a
     Decolonial somewhere
To your being. How can I know
     Something different without
Tracing something different? How
     Do I build from a corroded base?

V.

My three languages are colonized.
     Como serpientes me envuelven,

A patchwork of scales and skin.
     Me asusta la fuerza de mi voz,

My sharp words cause ruptures
     En nepantla pero esa palabra

Is not mine to claim, not mine.
     Quisiera tanto tener comunidad,

To know the original source
     Mi cultura pero nunca lo sabré.

I search inside my own becoming
     Busco mi pasado en lo que seré.

Convivir does not mean to live together

En español, love has gradations. *Te quiero pero no te amo,*
says a teenage boy trying to have it both ways.
La güera is your light-skinned prima.
El gringo is that white man
who mispronounces two phrases in español
and expects to be praised like he recited
a García Lorca poem by heart.

Mojado is an immigrant who survives
coyotes, la migra y ese maldito río.
Deserves a towel, chocolate, and a fireplace
to take the chill from the bones.
Aunque ahora es el desierto que toma
el agua, la piel y los sueños de los migrantes.

Cuando se me caía la mollera, the curandera
did not massage me, me sobaba.
She would draw espiritus from me with an egg,
rub the huevo against me like an elegy to syncretism,
to Purépecha gods I can never pray to
because I do not know their names.

The times my monolingual father called me a pendejo,
it hurt worse than all the English curse words
I learned in elementary school combined.
When the word pendejo leaves the lips of my papá,
it means I am a failure y nunca seré nada.
¿Cómo se dice therapy en español?

I no longer dream in Spanish.
My nightmares are in English.
But when I cry o doy mi corazón,
lo hago en two different tongues.

The Face Off

My father stared Death in the face and
made him laugh

Afterward they went off together
for a drink

It was my father's first drink
in two Cancer years

To Dream is to Mourn

I.

The walls of the barn rot hungrily
Butcher hooks decorate
My body like lights
On a Christmas tree
Shallow light bounces off
My father's crutches
Seeing me he lifts
Himself to his feet
Hugs a support beam
My father knows he will die
He falls to the ground
Spinal cord shatters
Flames birth flames
Scorch the darkness
I offer my broken body
My father is incandescent

II.

A worn park bench sits
Cradling my father
And me on the shoreline
We look across emerald waves
Toward a man-made fiefdom
A thick layer of white feces claims
The island for the birds
Moldy bread brings the flock
Like a gentle poison
Frenzy ensues decisively,
My father snatches
A pigeon in rough hands
Pulls a pocket knife

I notice fishing line
Snaked around each crease
Of the pigeon's feet
Two completed amputations
Three in progress
I search the ground for pigeon toes
My father cuts and untangles
He shows me groves
Not unlike those that cover
His body
He lets the pigeon fly
My father staggers on his crutches

I go lucid
All my questions
Flock into my mind
I am not vessel

Enough to contain them
I open my mouth
Feathers, beaks, and claws gurgle
In my throat
I shut my mouth
Listen
My father
Does not know
He is dead.

III.

Atop a writhing sea a black
Granite base balances
There, escalators point to nowhere
Run perpendicular

My father waits in his wheelchair
I sail to him on a raft
Around my neck is a chain,
An anchor for my vessel

Holographic doors open
I push my father into the sea
He rematerializes behind me
Won't let me touch him

He will not let me hold.

Retrofitting Bridges: Tales of a Lost Soul in the Third Space

I came to you (myself) at a time of unmitigated confusion.
Wind and rain enveloped me like a
ghostly cloak.

I need you to love me even when you hate me.

My skin cracks   and ruptures
into heart-shaped snowflakes.

They shatter into sand, a dust as brittle as identity.

I add love
to insult.

Stir in hate
with a dash of
consciousness
and bake to perfection.

I used to feed
you mediocrity.
Now you revel at
being consumed
by a utopia that will
always remain
a potentiality.

I retrofit bridges
                    because my life depends on it.
My being is fused to the structures.

                              As I step onto them,
sections of concrete instantaneously
combust around me.

          I have lost count of the number of times
                              I have drowned trying to cross.

I am in a perennial state of healing myself and my bridges.
But I continue to do so.

                    I
                  hate
                 myself
                because
                    I
                 cannot
                  write
                  this.

I am trapped in the

                    in-between,
                              but I am at home in this third-space

for it is the space where I was born, where I grew up, and where I
continue to live.

At this moment I am changing.

My cells are dying and being reborn.

My neurons cyclone trying to remember the
sensation of being alive. I am

the shaman and the hexed.

The witnessed and the invisible.

I am building an army.

I have drafted hundreds of thousands complete with

heavy artillery,

bullets, and

grenades.

With this	my army of
letters	words
will	terrorize,
destroy	assumptions
I will	bombard.

You are not just you. You are a culmination of every book, limestone,
conspiracy, oppression, empathy, and all else you have experienced.
You have taken from every person just as you have given.

On this day I want you to know that I love you,

especially when I hate you.

I run from myself and my body aches

I smash mirrors. No eye wear protects me from my crafting. I
am adobe sun amalgamation, straw and dirt. Heat becomes itself
on asphalt. Stomach rolls like a landscape. Angles are a national
monument. My joints naturally begin to decompose. Family medical
history hunts   like a leopard. Consume   the body as
something to hide. With   so much mutation   why can't
I be superhuman? Instead, scalpels are the paint brushes of my future.
Body as calamity, as breathless canvas. I shorten my life with pleasures.
Only mangled steel away from expiration. What if my cuts never
healed? Would I slice myself like an   invitation?
I turn into desiring object desired, jagged shards gnawing at my
reflection.

Specificity

Let me tell you about
a butterfly kiss
from dragon's wings,
about future huskies,
Soccer cleats encased in mud,
penguins facing gale-force
winds in shifts.

If you chose
tell me your terrors.
How they walk,
the color of their hair,
do they have siblings?
Mine do.

I will give you tiny mirrors
like random jellybeans
on the tongue.

I've walked upon
the Mexican cobblestones
of my parents' love story.

I once fed a baby chick
half a scorpion,
sat with the chick on my lap
until final breath.

Have you ever seen
a Mendocino tide pool?
Crabs basking in sunlight
as if they have no
natural predators.

Recall: the universal
is power's capillaries,
an iron maiden
that peers and flexes.

No matter how I stretch
I find iron in every direction.
Spikes plunge
Themselves
Into my body.
My blood dissolves
Metal like hydrochloric acid.
We become liquid together.

A Chicano Checks Into his Hotel Room

He sits fixated on an overly thick lampshade.
Hand-stitched ambient light.

Even his daydreams here are expensive.
Wings shine from a disproportionate chandelier.

The opulence casually bruises him.
He gets up to check into his room.

The manager sets down keys on the counter,
already looking past him to the next customer.

"Thank you!" he replies in a high-pitched voice
coupled with a practiced, extra smile.

Then comes the shiver. Patrons and patrons and looks.
"Why?" the silence seems to ask.

He swipes the cardkey, a blind click welcomes him.
He finds the same blackout curtains, the same flat screen,

but also the same bed with the goose down pillows,
with the 1,000 thread-count Egyptian cotton sheets.

He sets down his duffel bag, removes his clothes
along with the residue of carbon dioxide and noxious eyes.

He lays on the right-hand edge of the king-sized bed,
like when he shared a twin-sized bed with his brother.

He sleeps deeply, reveling at the thought that this space
was not made for him.

On my break from teaching Spanish

Two cop cars block the street where I parked my 1996 Volvo
One police officer looks through my car's windows
According to the officer holding my license my car
Matches the description but I don't have
The demeanor of someone who would shoot
Another someone in a fit of road rage.

To Those That Came

Before me, I see dandelions
displayed like jewelry.
Each atop a hand
carved wooden stand.
I blow into each in turn.
Some make declarations, some scream
or roar, some converse and others lecture,
others say nothings
in the ear.
Upstairs I examine
the stems. I run
my thumb making
out letters by touch.
Gasps escape as I recognize
the names. I gust through the room.
Heave oxygen like discordant
chatter. Seeds float, linger
like a San Francisco fog.
I collapse on the hardwood
floor, starfish while
covered in seeds looking
up at a roof that is
older than my particular
constellation of atoms.
I try to imagine my whispers
floating nimbus across
countries, worlds.
The impossibility closes

my eyes. In the darkness
behind my eyelids
the dandelion seeds light up
like city lights welcoming
me back
into the night.

Stroll at Night

My presence marred
the sacred vigil
of phantom millions.
A barrier of dark
trees kissed a wisp
of startled air with ecstasy.
The colossal vitality
of their illusions
made a shadow
on the unquiet darkness
as wind does the sea.
They were consumed
with wonder at a labyrinth
of windshields
that dispensed starlight
to casual moths.
Hot whips of panic
traveled through my body
like a star to the moon. With the flash
of a waving hand,
I left the moonlight,
watching over nothing.

Letter to the white people who realized their lives are also expendable when in the service of capitalism (circa March 2020)

Trump wants U.S. economy 'opened up and raring to go' by Easter
—John Wagner and Brady Dennis, *Washington Post*

When our president says he'd kill you
part of me wishes I could turn back time
so I could preserve your innocence
a moment longer.
You see, I'm used to my body being
considered a threat. To be called
a burden while carrying the brunt.
You have little practice. Like a cub
you put your paw into the fire
for too long. I understand
your desire to call the flame light,
to call your burns something
other than a warning.
I too yearned for safety
from those positioned
to offer it, then was accused
of crimes solely because of my name,
because of my skin.
I have seen others succumb
to their own denial.
I have seen the cautious

thrown into the blaze.
Now you see we are already burning.
When I say I want us to live,
I mean I want us to live.

Politics

Talking heads swear *church*,
restless moths drown
in the honey. I fear
like the tenderness

behind a cobra's hood.
But terrors aren't allowed
to cry. Dragonfly says *clip my hindwings*
like a promise. Loss is no more

than a habitat.
Theatre thaws,
sheds dividends to the zealous.
Larvae promises *I can burrow through*

the skin. Please do not renounce me,
draw from me instead.

Elegy for Jakelin

7-year-old Guatemalan girl who died in Border Patrol custody is identified ...

Each day I open class with a morning circle.
Nineteen 7- and 8-year-olds sit
on a colorful rug. Talk about
their favorite color,
ideal superpowers, how they feel
or who they will be when they grow up.
I tell them I wish I could teleport. Cross
walls without a second thought. Be
one blink away from my family.
At recess I read about a 7-year-old
who died in Border Patrol custody
after navigating the New Mexican desert.
Her name is Jakelin Caal Maquin.
I begin to wonder:
Did she make walking through the desert a game?
Count the number of cacti. Make
messages with stones in the sand.
I wonder if she went to school.
Did she have to leave midway
through the year to work
picking strawberries
or donkey dung to sell
like my father?
I imagine my classroom with 20 students.
Would she color in desert sunrises?

Or would the deep sunset reds and oranges
be her inspiration. I wonder
if she knew where she was going.
What was America to her? I wonder
if she spoke K'iche' or English or Spanish or Mam.
What would she write about?
One of my students wrote,
Another word for ordinary is God.
I prep the math Do Now on the white board.
My students are learning multiplication.
I wonder if she knew her times tables.
What is 15,000 children times two parents
in a different detention facility?
My students know any number of bottles of water
times Border Patrol boots equals zero.
Did she know the definition of terror,
or did she call it fear?
The not knowing tears.

Built to Mourn

Sometimes I convince   myself

I was built   to mourn

programmed   by mitochondrial

DNA   or perhaps   conditioned   by scarcity

I mourn the past   the chances

not taken   the healing   postponed

parental sacrifices   to unmeritocratic gods

subjugation of   my ancestors

by my ancestors

my blood   strangles itself

my dead   and yours

I mourn the present   inability to stay

in this moment   here

the children murdered   here

the nation   -less   can populate   their own   planet

wilting bookstores   artesanía shops

news as myth-making   with no protagonist

systems are   the only demi-gods

emperor penguins   collapse into

our inequity

I mourn the future   humanity

as self-destructive

sinking cities

commodified   filtered tears

my life   as fiction
          the earth   wants
                    to forget   but scabs
persist

          mis hijos   mis hijos   mis hijos
                forgive me   for what
                          I drowned

III

Letter to Future Self

Dearest me, do you still
Live? Is sunlight still a thing?

Is your cannibalism radioactive
Or still capitalist?

Are your body and your city submerged
Underwater? Crabs eat gourmet epidermis.

Is your society post-racial?
Just kidding, I know
It's not post-racial.

Have you learned to sit
Your mind still?

Do you still forget your
Dreams like dimes into a wishing well?

Does your body let you
Self-care? How broken

Is too broken? Are you still broken?
Are we?

I offer you my mistakes
Like handcuffs. Best forget

Yours, truly.

Surviving the Desert

The remains of at least 2,832 migrants have been found in southern Arizona since 2001, according to the Arizona OpenGIS Initiative for Deceased Migrants. Nearly 40 percent (1,089) have never been identified.

—**Daniel Gonzalez**, *USA Today Network*

Anger blossoms in the Sonoran Desert
burrowing like a scorpion awaiting the
crepuscular. Here the shadows plant
desert marigolds in shallow graves,
exhale dry sweat as divots collect on the
fracture. How could anything survive?
Gaunt prickly pear cactus struggles
haggardly to keep itself from slouching.
Inside, a cactus wren hides from the
jaws of heat waves searing green flesh.
Kilometers of road stretch like a tongue,
like a lit fuse. Even the paths are thirsty.
Moisture, that molecular god, shines upon
nocturnal prey. Temporary respite, the dark
offers the fiction of the opaque. Return to the
plaza with its festive colors like the
quetzal in flight, belly emblazoned with
rivers of fire. Stars guide towards possibility,
skeletal and otherwise. The bones anchor
time like an unwilling beast chained to the
umbra of an eclipsing moon. Hear the

voices chant their cerulean song:
What of tenderness? Call it dried
xerophyte. Call it drowning fish. Let it
yearn until its desperation reaches its
zenith then watch it plunge into the sand.

The children who die in custody have names

Children are being separated from their families Children are dying at the border Children are waking up in dirt tents in the desert Children are living in a former WWII Japanese internment camps Children includes babies Children includes toddlers in tender age shelters Children are not being processed quickly Children are not being medically screened properly Children are not receiving adequate medical care Children are being treated like criminals Children are forgetting who their parents are Children are rejecting the parents who were powerless to prevent separation Children are screaming "You are not my mother!" Children are dying in ICE custody Children are dying in Border Patrol custody Children are generating profit for private prisons Children are being lost in the system Children are being sexually abused Children are slipping through cracks Children are being held in cages Children are being targeted to create a living hell for immigrants Children are dying at the border Children are dying at the border Children are dying at the border Children are dying at the border Children are dying die Children are the future the future dying

7-year-old migrant girl taken into Border Patrol custody dies of dehydration, exhaustion
Jakelin Caal Maquin

8-Year-Old Migrant Boy Dies In Government Custody In New Mexico Hospital
Felipe Gomez Alonso

'He Went Seeking Life But Found Death.' How a Guatemalan Teen Fleeing Climate Change Ended Up Dying in a U.S. Detention Center
Juan de León Gutiérrez

Toddler apprehended at the U.S.-Mexico border dies after weeks in hospital
Wilmer Josué Ramírez Vásquez

16-year-old migrant boy dies in U.S. custody, 5th child to die since December
Carlos Gregorio Hernandez Vasquez

A Toddler's Death Adds To Concerns About Migrant Detention
Mariee Juárez

CBP identifies 10-year-old girl who died in US custody in September
Darlyn Cristabel Cordova-Valle

11-year old buy dies after spending 6 days in a Border Patrol Detention Center
Gustavo Barahona-López

My shadow tells me not to hide in the darkness

Build self   upon   me.   Make me

          terror or   justification

or game.   I fold and   breach

          like water.   Move   me vascular.

               I dance,   ritual.   Make me

puppets.   I pinball   through

          vocal   cords,   I seep

          into tongue.   Keep mouth   half

     open.   I bind   to others.   My body

          as absentee bridge.   Hold me

close   but don't let me

               inside.   I am all   fears,

history,   and   shape.   You

          cast yourself   too deep,   too deep.

The skeleton goes to the supermarket

On a day like any other the skeleton decides to go to the supermarket. He stows away his reusable bag in his ribs to save another small piece of a faraway tree. At the store he sees aisles full of cans. Tomatoes and peaches and all sorts of legumes. Every can is well past its expiration date. The skeleton takes a can of vegetable broth and goes in search of fish. As he looks over the selection, the skeleton imagines what the cartilage would look like clothed in flesh and scales. After choosing the fish with the emptiest eye sockets, the skeleton walks slowly to pay for his groceries. The skeleton smiles at a bony cashier as he takes a charred twenty-dollar bill out of his duct tape wallet. The bill turns to dust when it touches the cashier's fingers. The cashier doesn't bat an eye.

License to Live

In the warm, afternoon
light, the migrant tore
open an envelope,
and found a glistening
license, stamped with
the dancing letters,
D-M-V.
After he carefully placed
the laminated treasure
into his skinny
wallet, he grabbed
his keys and flew
into a car, barely a grade
above a jalopy.
Without the usual fear,
he let the vehicle roar,
after all, he was official.

But that was years ago
and the faded letters no longer danced,
and the card was expired.
But at last the migrant gave the license
to his son, who in turn put it
into a skinny wallet they purchased together
at a flea market.

And the son, trying to remember
his father's face, often stared into

his father's laminated eyes.
The son pulled
at the memories trapped inside
the holographic image
the way we all long to recall
even a small piece of
that someone that we have lost.

Bond

Once,   you broke my earth   open.
      Brought down my constellations   with a slingshot,
        Planted seeds in   the nape of my neck,
Poured spirit   down my throat.

With you,   I sing new stars into being.
       I nourish saplings into   forests spanning my back.
        I drink of you   like a communion.
    With me, you let your fire burn incandescent.

     You blast dams leaving nascent   waterfalls in your wake.
You remember you are enough.
          Once, you rip me open.
      You make me roll up my skin   (scars and all)

Like the poster   for a movie you would never
      Watch.   You make me leave   myself behind
   Like a carcass scavenged clean by your need
      Of me.   Do you love me enough not to

         Kill me?   Is that your way of letting go?
I tear you to shreds once
      Maybe twice   or three times.   I watch
    You through the prism of   my own cuts.   Resist

The urge   to collect your ribbons   and make you
     Whole again.   I tell you your smile   is the cruelest

Of promises.   I berate you   with my silence.
But once I speak,   I mend us.   Or maybe

You do the mending   this time.   Out of this thread
        We make our specters.

Tenderness

At this hour she sleeps like a shoreline, the soothing tide of
her breath whispers. She lies upon, under, next to, and above a
meticulously placed pod of pillows. They swim with her in watery
dreams. He snores, sprawled in every direction like a random rock
formation. Suddenly, he rolls into himself taking the comforter with
him. She half-wakes as her practiced arm pulls at her share of the
bedding. With no warmth forthcoming, she begins to boil. With
one well-placed shove he goes tumbling like a rockslide. She screams,
jumps out, throwing pillows with abandon. As she is rounding the
bed, she sees he is still passed out cold. When the relief passes she
taps him on the shoulder, *You took all the covers!* she snarls like a
storm tearing at a window pane. With his eyes still shut he answers,
Don't you have to get ready to go to King's Landing? He nuzzles his
cheek onto the blue carpet. He wakes to find her wrapped around
him, a layer of blankets on them like freshly fallen snow. He kisses
her cheek and lays his head on the ground,
awaiting the tyranny of the alarm bell's sound.

Smiles

I sit under a cork oak watching
my son in his portable playpen.

Light swerves past leaves
projecting ghosts like
stained glass. I adjust the canopy
on the playpen.

My son bites
his teething ring
with gusto
and coats of slobber.

He grabs fistfuls of mesh
netting, pulls himself up
on his bare feet, and falls.

He rolls onto his tummy looking
for his next distraction.

My son stares at people passing by
curiously, flashing gummy smiles.
The strangers smile back.

Reflexively, I smile too.
But once the people are out
of sight
and my smile fades,

I think about the country
my son was born into.

Babies, not much older than my son
are separated from their parents.

I recall a video of a family
reunited where the son yells
at his mother that he has
no mother.

I think too of strangers.
How at all times
part of my mind is prepared
to have the cops called on me.

Will strangers mark my son's body
as a threat too?
Will his bilingual tongue make him
somehow less American in their eyes?

My son notices I am no longer
with him so he lets out
a cry. He raises two little
arms above his head
in my direction.

I pick him up and hold him facing me
then smile, and coo, and cry at once.

Dew Drops

Today, my baby cries
like I cried when
I saw the photograph.
A father and toddler
floating like fallen leaves
on the banks of the Río
Grande.
My fingers follow my child's
outstretched arms.
I raise my son like the
present, like a promise.
His cheeks collect dew
like tulip petals.
Our noses touch,
he smiles wide
when dew drops
roll into his lip.
I did not know
grief and joy
could be held
in the same smile.

There is a Ghost in my House

There is a ghost in my house.
He does not make lights
flicker or move
objects or make noises
in the night.
He does not try to scare
people by appearing
at inopportune moments.
He lives and lets live.

He wonders what is
really behind the light
and when he should cross
into it. Likes to stream
"The Exorcist" on the family
Netflix account although demons
scare him and exorcisms
seem inconvenient.

He wishes his father had
not gotten cancer
and that they had shared
a proper goodbye
before each became a ghost
of what they had once been.
Curse family
histories. A father,

son, and holy
spirit gone.

I have a ghost
in my house
but I don't want him
to leave, because right
now things feel
safe and familiar.
But he feels empty,
transparent
and so I am afraid
that I will lose
him again.

Quarantine Meditation

After Rona Luo

Close your eyes, feel the sensation,
your clothes against your body.
I close my eyes and gift my nerve-
endings all of my attention.
Feel the sensation of the air
touching your skin.
My child envelops his toddler
hand around my pinky.
Visualize a white light,
follow it through the forest.
My child pulls me away
saying *Come, come.*
Cross the river, you see your
ancestor on the shoreline.
I glance at my face on Zoom,
see my past in my features.
Your ancestor gives you a gift:
an object, a hug, a few words.
My father gifts me his eyes,
I stare into our hazel irises.
Return to the forest, listen
to the leaves. What do you see?
My child climbs on me and
stands upright on my thigh.
My arms ready themselves to catch
but my child does not waver.

They call us fence-hoppers, we call ourselves skywalkers

We began to incubate our wings to reach
the sun. Before any tea parties or unifications,
before the first fingers curled around a flag pole.
We practiced collecting mangoes with no ladders,
climbed smoke to harvest pearls from the sky.
Each night we delighted in picking cobwebs
out of each other's hair.

Now, the gateway to the earth, the heavens
is ajar to us. We drink water with our eyes.
Rivers will never devour us.
Joining hands, we synchronize
our flight patterns. Rocket
towards the moon like Apollo.

They call us locusts forgetting
how we have fed them.
Our drums are their thunder,
our sabotage is their sublime.
Their failure is not our responsibility,
yet we reach out to them still.

Our children use walls as volleyball nets,
switch sides at each half.
Our children project themselves upon
deserts, pouring smiles down as if the cacti
hold cameras in the sheer of their needles.

We play hide and seek among the clouds,
sculpt them into phoenix feathers. We chase
each other over mountains and into valleys
knowing we chose when to return to the earth.

Home, a Becoming

I remind myself that my legs are countries. The way
Borders are the hemlines of worn jeans.

How do you say goodbye to backyard pomegranates?
They demand remittances like body parts.

Lips and arms and cheeks to be kissed by a monarch
Butterfly. I rip off the barbed wire across my spine,

Protection for the casa triste that lives on my temple.
How do you greet America? Like a lost lover

Torn from you by time or lust or hate?
Like a child not at peace with self?

I become the orchard and the railroad. I raise
The children, bury the dead. I make myself

A home. I build connection like water creates
Caverns, writing names on stone walls.

Weathering

Torrential rain silences
The unmaking of desert dunes.
Cactus throat swells
And I call it love.

Love, that clash
Of clouds, that smell
Of slipping touch.

Love takes refuge
On the snake's fallow
Tongue. Sand overfills
Its own wanting.

Love carries the
Body's minerals
In its vanishing light.

The waiting too
Is love. The drought
And the flood. The thirst
And the drowning.

Let me be ground
Water enough
To quench the unseen.
Let us lick
The purple
From the sky.

About the Art

Autorretrato como hechicera, 2023.
Hand-dyed paper on paper, 9" x 24".
Art by Sofia Moreno

Acknowledgements

I am extremely grateful to the literary magazines and anthologies that gave my poems their first homes.

Azahares; Quarterly West; Kissing Dynamite; Iron Horse Literary Review; Marias at Sampaguitas; Lunch Ticket; Feral; Oxford Review of Books; PALABRITAS; Homology Lit.; Fourteen Hills; Trampset; Hobart After Dark; Hayden's Ferry Review; Acentos Review; Rattle; Glass Poetry; Puerto del Sol; Moonchild Magazine; Apogee; Into the Void

Anthologies:
No Tender Fences: an Anthology of Immigrant & First Generation American Poetry to Raise Funds for RAICES-Texas; Puro Chicanx Writers of the 21st Century; Crossing Lines: An anthology of immigrant poetry; Broken Sleep Books: Immigrant Poetry Anthology; Até Mais: a Latinx Futurisms Anthology.

Thank you to my writing community. This accomplishment, the publishing of a debut full-length collection, would not have been possible without your support, guidance, and example. For someone who did not attend an MFA program, having exceptional writers and friends believe in me and my work cannot be overstated. I am particularly grateful to Muriel Leung, Alan Chazaro, Jerry Flores, Marcelo Hernandez Castillo, Preeti Vangani, Jenny Qi, Rosebud Ben-Oni, Dorothy Chan, Jose Hernandez Diaz, Raina J. León, Hector son of Hector, and Gustavo Hernandez. Your feedback and support have been invaluable.

To my sister, Yesi, and brother, Alex, thank you for always being there for me. I love you both dearly.

Thank you to my little humans, Romero and Issa, for bringing so much joy into my life and inspiring me to pursue my literary dreams. I hope I make you both proud.

Thank you to my partner, Kati Barahona-López, for being my first reader, making time and space for my creative work, and being a general badass. You are my role model and every day I strive to be a little more like you. Thank you for navigating life with me. I love you.

Mamá, gracias por darme la vida y por darme la confianza y el apoyo necesario para sobresalir. La quiero muchísimo.

Papá, no pasa un solo día sin que yo piense en usted. Más de una década después de su muerte el dolor sigue allí, evolucionando y persistiendo. Aunque nuestra relación fue compleja nunca he dudado de su amor por mi. Lo quiero y lo extraño tanto.

And finally to you dear reader, thank you for spending time with my foundations.

About the Author

Gustavo Barahona-López is a writer and educator from Richmond, California. In his writing, Barahona-López draws from his experience growing up as the son of Mexican immigrants. He was a finalist for the 2021 Quarterly West poetry prize and his chapbook *Loss and Other Rivers That Devour* was published by Nomadic Press in 2022. A VONA alum, Barahona-López's work can be found or is forthcoming in *Iron Horse Literary Review, Puerto del Sol, The Acentos Review, Apogee Journal,* and *Hayden's Ferry Review*, among other publications.

FLOWERSONG
PRESS

FlowerSong Press nurtures essential verse from, about, and throughout the borderlands. Literary. Lyrical. Boundless.

Sign up for announcements about
new and upcoming titles at:

www.flowersongpress.com

www.ingramcontent.com/pod-product-compliance
Lightning Source LLC
Chambersburg PA
CBHW031447120626
46545CB00006B/2595